INSIDE STORY

TELEVISION

by TIM BYRNE and TONY GREGORY

Wayland

INSIDE STORY

Football
Pop Music
Fashion
Motor Racing
Teen Magazines
Television

First published in 1989 by Wayland (Publishers) Limited
61 Western Road, Hove, East Sussex BN3 1JD.

Cover: The hilarious comediennes Dawn French (top) and Jennifer Saunders.
Apart from their own successful BBC2 series, Dawn and Jennifer have acted in
Happy Families and the *Comic Strip* productions.

Editor: Deborah Elliott
Designer: Helen White

British Library Cataloguing in Publication Data
Byrne, Tim
1. Great Britain. Television services
I. Title II. Gregory, Tony
384.55'4'0941

ISBN 1-85210-711-1

CONTENTS

CHAPTER ONE

THE
PRODUCTION TEAM

Television is one of the most powerful forms of the media. The visual images that we are presented with on our television screens can often influence and persuade us much more than the written word. To have a career in television is one of the most popular ambitions among people of all ages. It offers glamour, the opportunity to work with famous and interesting people and, generally, high wages. More than all this, however, it offers the prospect of very hard work.

Television is a diverse and complex industry. The range of different programmes made includes news, drama, comedy, films, documentaries, children's, nature and music. All the programmes are very different and involve different types of people and different methods of production.

Because so many people find the idea of working in television appealing, competition for jobs is very tough. You can give yourself an advantage by gaining experience in a parallel industry first, such as newspapers, magazines, theatre or radio. However, it may take a while, even then, to break into television. The thing to keep in mind is persistence.

Specific types of programme appeal to a particular age group or type of person. *Top of the Pops* and *The Chart Show* are aimed at young people who like pop music, whereas a programme about opera is usually aimed at older people who like classical music. The first thing for you to decide, if you want to work in television, is the type of programme you want to work on. Those people who have been lucky and dedicated enough to get into the television industry and establish a career for themselves, must always be aware of certain things: who exactly the audience the programmes are being aimed at are, and what that audience wants to see. The television industry is there to please the public.

THE PROGRAMME DEVISER

The programme deviser's role is to come up with ideas for television programmes. Once a programme deviser has thought of an idea, he or she has to put it down on paper in a programme format. This is a document which sets out in detail how the programme will be structured and what it will be about. A programme format has to be quite long and must show that all the ideas have been properly thought out. It must also contain a mock running order and script.

Once a programme format has been written it has to be submitted to a television company. The best person to send a programme format to is the head of a department, such as the head of the current affairs or children's department. A television committee will then meet to decide whether or not the programme should be commissioned. Sometimes a 'one-off' pilot programme is made to see if the idea works or not and if the viewing public respond to it favourably. If a programme is commissioned then a large team of people are brought together to actually put the programme 'on air' (broadcast the programme on television).

John Dale is a programme deviser for TVS. He came up with the ideas for two successful Saturday morning children's programmes, *Number 73* and *Motormouth*.

▲ Liverpudlian Phil Redmond devised two popular and successful television series. BBCI's Grange Hill *is set in a comprehensive school and realistically portrays the problems of everyday life faced by young people. Phil Redmond has included controversial issues such as dyslexia, rape, AIDS and divorce in* Brookside *(Channel 4). This twice-weekly soap opera is centred around a group of people living in Liverpool.*

The way in: According to John Dale: *'Often the best way to think up an idea for a programme is from outside television itself. Working with young people can help you understand what they are interested in and like to do. What you must do is put yourself in their position and think of the sort of things they would like to see on television. What you really need is a TV company that is willing to do two things - take a risk and invest money in an idea.'*

What the job involves: *'Being a programme deviser is not really a 9am to 5pm job. It's having good, original ideas, which can come to you at any time of the day or night. What you really have to be good at is communicating your ideas to other people.'*

THE RESEARCHER

A television researcher's job is to come up with ideas and items that can go into individual programmes.

Researchers also have to follow these ideas up by contacting relevant people, checking material and generally making sure that all the ideas are original and will work on screen. Many ideas that seem good in theory or that look good on paper, do not necessarily translate to the television screen. Researchers often have to go out 'on the road' to meet the people involved in the item. Researchers need to be sociable and self-confident, because so much of their job involves dealing with people and asking pertinent questions to get the exact information they want. If an item involves an object or a display, then researchers have to check everything out. A good television researcher must be prepared to investigate every detail and every possible eventuality, especially for live television programmes.

Researchers have to work out the structure of an item before it appears on the programme. They write notes describing the item for the producer, actors and presenters. All items have to be approved by the producer before they can go ahead. The producer, presenters, actors and researchers meet to discuss the items and how they should be presented. Together they decide what to say and when, how to introduce guests, what questions to ask and how to bring an item to an end.

Television is all about team work and team effort. No one individual can make, create and put a programme on air.

▲ Jonathon Ross began his career in television as a researcher. He now hosts the popular Channel 4 chat show The Last Resort.

Researchers have to work closely with the director, set designer, computer graphics designer, make-up artist, wardrobe assistant, sound engineer and stage management team.

On the actual day, when the programme is to be recorded or broadcast live, researchers have to do a number of things.

● Meet the guests.

● Show the guests to their dressing rooms and keep them entertained.

● Take them to the make-up department and to the studio.

● Rehearse the item with the guest and presenter.

● Make sure the guest is relaxed and confident and will not 'dry up' in front of the camera.

● Make sure that all the people and items due to appear in the show are ready.

● Answer telephone calls from viewers.

▲ Working as a television researcher means spending most of your time making telephone calls — finding and checking out potential guests and items, setting up meetings etc — trying to come up with interesting and original ideas for your particular programme, and meetings with the producer to discuss your ideas. Although essentially it is an office job, there are opportunities to go 'on the road' to meet people.

Sarah West is a television researcher who has worked on programmes such as *Number 73, Get Fresh, Telethon* and *Motormouth*.

The way in: Sarah West says: *'I started off working for a fringe theatre in London. I saw an advert in a newspaper for a TV researcher and I answered it. The programme wanted someone who knew about the cabaret and light entertainment scene in London. I did, so I was perfect for the job.'*

What the job involves:
To be a good researcher, you must:

● have a good memory.

● be good at finding people and information.

● be good at talking to people on the telephone.

● be very interested and committed to the programme and items you work on.

THE PRODUCER

A producer is someone who is responsible for the content of a television programme, including features, guests and stories - in fact, absolutely everything that goes into a programme.

Producers are also responsible for managing the people who work on a programme - presenters, actors, scriptwriters and researchers. They also have the final say in the clothes the presenters wear and the way a story or item is shaped. On news programmes, producers are sometimes called 'editors', because their job is similar to that of a newspaper editor.

Producers have to put together a running order which shows in what order features will take place and how long they will last. Producers also check every word that the presenters or actors are going to say.

John Morrell has produced many programmes for the BBC, including *Panorama, That's Life, Watchdog* and *Newsnight*.

▲ *The production gallery of BBCI's* The Wogan Show. *The producer (left) checks through her running order to make sure the live programme is keeping to its schedule.*

8

The way in: According to John Morrell: *'I always wanted to be a writer, so I gained a lot of experience for television as a journalist on local papers. I eventually worked for the Daily Telegraph. I moved into television by becoming a researcher for the BBC. Eventually, I became a producer on news programmes.'*

So you want to be a producer?

● It would be useful to have a university, polytechnic or college education.

● Gain experience as a journalist on local papers or in local radio.

● If you are lucky enough to get a job in television, work your way up through the ranks by gaining experience as a researcher or television journalist.

● You must be a good team manager and be able to understand people and their ideas. You must also be good at communicating your ideas in a confident and positive way.

Julia Smith, former producer of the successful Eastenders *soap opera, is photographed here in fictional Albert Square with Roly — the dog from 'The Queen Vic'.* Eastenders *proved one of the television phenomena of the 1980s, bringing to its 20 million regular viewers issues like drug abuse, cot death, schoolgirl pregnancy, disability and racism. These, and other issues, confronted by Julia Smith's series, are often ignored by mainstream television programmes.* Eastenders *continues with its policy of reflecting the good and the bad of modern life.*

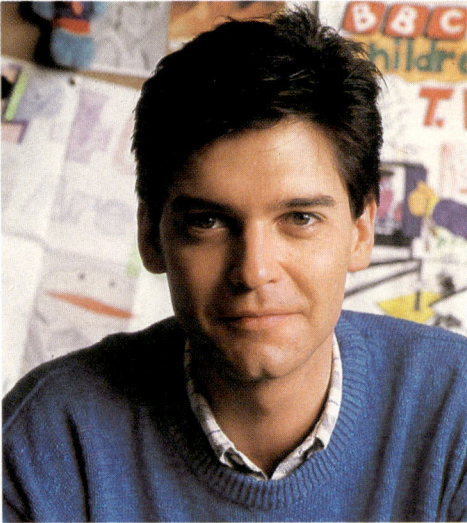

Philip Schofield is one of the most popular people on television and is the idol of many young people. His natural, easy-going manner and professionalism helped to make the Saturday morning children's programme Going Live a success.

THE PRESENTER

There are many types of television presenter, from news readers to flamboyant game show hosts. Different personalities and approaches are suited to different types of programme. It would be difficult to imagine a serious news item being read by Les Dawson, or Channel 4's trendy *The Last Resort* being presented by Paul Daniels. The actual job of a presenter, however, is basically the same – to present things on screen.

Presenters need to be confident and good at communicating, so that viewers can understand what they are talking about and remain interested. They also need to remain calm under all circumstances – no matter how unexpected. For example, if the link to an outside broadcast or film report goes wrong, the presenter has to ad lib and try to make things continue smoothly. This can often prove very difficult, as the presenter has to react immediately and in such a professional and natural way that the viewers will not realize anything is wrong. Imagine how stressful this must be!

◀ *In the early 1980s Muriel Gray presented the cult Channel 4 music programme* The Tube *with Paula Yates and Jools Holland. She went on to host* Frocks on the Box *with Marie Helvin, before returning to Channel 4 to present the popular* The Media Show.

BBC news reader Moira Stuart. Moira presents news from all over the world in a clear, interesting and unbiased manner. ▶

Very often presenters have to do more than one thing at a time. During the programme, when presenters are talking or interviewing guests, they are continually being fed talkback through a hidden earpiece. Talkback is messages from the production assistant (PA), director or producer, detailing, for example, how much time is left, what question to ask next, or what is happening next. Often, presenters also have to read an autocue. This is a machine which projects the script on to the camera lens, so the presenter can read it.

The way in: Tony Gregory has presented the youth shows *Network 7* and *Motormouth*. He says: *'My career began as a presenter on a small local radio station. I started off by filling in for the main presenters when they were on holiday. From that I learnt basic presentation skills.'* Tony actually got his first 'lucky break' into the world of television thanks to the Channel 4 programme *Network 7*. This popular and 'revolutionary' youth programme was one of the first to adopt a lively, magazine approach and give the television public the opportunity to voice their opinions on certain issues. Each fast-moving item would inter-cut with another, and the young, fashionable presenters introduced, often controversial, items such as: Should we bring back the death penalty? and Should Ronnie Biggs (the 'Great Train Robber') be pardoned? Viewers could ring a telephone line and cast their votes.

Many presenters come from unlikely backgrounds. Muriel Gray has presented *The Tube*, *Frocks on the Box* and *The Media Show*. How did her break come about? *'I was in a band in Edinburgh and working as a civil servant in a museum. The band hoped to be auditioned for* The Tube*, but somehow I ended up auditioning to be a presenter. When I was offered the job, I didn't initially want to do it. It was more or less just a hobby to start with, and then I just decided to make it a career.'*

So you want to be a presenter?

● Confidence is essential — you must not be afraid to talk in front of a camera. It is particularly important when conducting an interview to know how to talk to people and to always appear interested in what they have to say.

● You must be self-disciplined. Presenters often have to spend a couple of days in an office working hard on a script and planning questions for interviews. They have to rely on the knowledge of the researchers and trust the decisions of studio personnel, like floor managers and directors.

● Producers look for different people to present different types of programmes. Work out what your particular style of presentation is and which type of programme you would be most suited to present.

THE ACTOR

For many people the most glamorous role in television is that of the actor. A vast number of people are involved in producing a programme, yet it is the actors who receive all the attention, limelight and, more often than not, the praise. The success and failure of most television programmes can also depend heavily on the performances of the actors. It does not matter how good a script is, if it is delivered badly then the programme is not likely to work. Also, television produces a number of very poor programmes that are very successful thanks to the dominant presence and ability of good actors.

▲ Lenny Henry as Delbert Wilkins in a scene from The Lenny Henry Show. Lenny's career began on ITV's New Faces. He has gone on to become one of Britain's most popular and successful comedians.

Many people dream of becoming actors, yet relatively few manage to 'make it'. There are a number of paths open to star-struck hopefuls. Many successful actors admit, however, that their particular paths opened thanks to 'lucky breaks'. For seven years Andrea Arnold played the character Dawn in the Saturday morning children's drama *Number 73*. She says: *'The way into acting came about by pure accident for me. I saw an advertisement in an actors' newspaper. Just for a laugh I applied. When I found out they wanted me for an audition, I just couldn't believe it! For the audition I had to do five minutes of anything I wanted. For my act I did an impression, sang, danced and even went up to the producer and tried to bribe him with a £5 note. I suppose it worked! I got the job and he even let me keep my £5!'*

Routines vary depending on the type of programme, but usually actors receive their scripts about a week before going into the studio to record the programme. They rehearse their lines and positions with the director and producer away from the distractions of busy television studios. (The BBC has a special building on the outskirts of London which is full of large rehearsal rooms.) At this stage the producer and director might make alterations to the script. Studio rehearsals take place the day before the drama is recorded or broadcast live. This is like the dress rehearsal of a stage play and is mainly for the benefit of technical departments, such as lighting, sound and cameras.

◀ *Some of the pupils and teachers from BBC1's* Grange Hill. *This long-running drama series is set in a 'typical' comprehensive school.*

Some television programmes are recorded long before they are shown on television. Actors on these programmes have more time to rehearse lines and scenes than actors who appear in soap operas which run 52 weeks of the year without fail. For the cast and production teams of programmes like *Eastenders, Coronation Street, The Bill, Brookside* and *Neighbours*, meeting the demanding schedules means learning lines quickly, having little time for rehearsals and recording for long hours every day of the week.

Actress Susan Tulley plays Michelle in *Eastenders*. She says of her job: *'It's hard work because you start very early and sometimes don't finish until the evening. Often the only day I have off is Sunday. We record one episode of Eastenders about six weeks before it appears on screen.'*

This demanding work schedule can sometimes lead to a lessening in quality of the acting or production. The long-running Central TV soap *Crossroads* was eventually taken off the air because of what some people felt was its inferior quality. The programme went out three, or sometimes four times every week, so there was often little time to rehearse properly or re-shoot scenes.

▲ *Actor Alex Papps plays Frank in the popular Australian soap opera* Home and Away. *The series follows the fortunes of a number of young people living with foster parents in Summer Bay.*

Kylie Minogue and ▶ *Jason Donovan who are Charlene and Scott Robinson in the popular Australian soap opera* Neighbours. *Both Kylie and Jason have taken advantage of their screen success to become pop stars. They have had hit records both individually and together.*

▲ *The Corkhill family from Brookside. During the series the family has had more than its share of problems, including Tracey's affair with a teacher and sexual harassment at work and the break-up of Billy's (centre) marriage.*

So you want to be an actor?

● Audition for parts in school plays or local dramatic society productions. (Your local library should have details of all the local dramatic societies.)

● If you are particularly keen to become an actor, find out about stage schools in your area. Many film and television actors began their careers at stage schools. Many offer scholarships to young people who show particular talent.

● Think about taking up drama classes at school. It is possible to do GCSE drama - if your school does not offer this option, think about doing it at an evening class.

● Andrea Arnold gives any would-be actor this piece of advice: *'Ordinary life is the best experience in learning how to act. Be determined, if you want it enough you'll get it. Don't listen to people who try to discourage you.'*

CHAPTER TWO

GETTING ON AIR

THE DIRECTOR

Rick Gardner has been a director for many years, working on *Top of the Pops, Superchamps* and *Motormouth*. He also directed the 1981 Royal Wedding, when his pictures were seen by nearly three quarters of a billion people around the world.

What the job involves: According to Rick: *'I'm at the helm. Sitting in the gallery (control room), I'm in charge of sound, cameras, lights, graphics, make-up, wardrobe, scenery and so on. On a big live show, I could be looking after more than 100 people. It's a team effort, I need to rely on everyone's skills. I work very closely with the PA (production assistant). He or she provides me with all the timing and information I need to run the programme. Directing on location usually means working with a smaller team and often only one camera, but I'm still in charge — things must run smoothly. I've got to make sure we've recorded all the shots I need, so that when I come to edit the recording the pictures and sound tell the story, or get the message across.'*

The way in: Directors usually work on one type of programme, for example, sport or news. Drama directors often start as stage managers in theatres, learning how stories can be staged and how to work with actors. Directors also need to understand the technical side of television. Many directors actually begin their careers as part of a camera crew or as vision mixers, where they learn about the equipment. Some start as floor managers and build up their knowledge of studio floor organization.

So you want to be a director?

- Find out more about how a programme is made. Try to visit your local television studios — see if you can watch a director at work.

- Decide what area of programming interests you — sport, music, drama etc.

- Most directors do not start until their late twenties at the earliest. Think about starting your career in a related job, where you will learn about production techniques — production assistant, floor manager, camera person, or presenter, for example.

Tony Newman, the director of The Wogan Show. *Tony has to make split-second decisions on camera angles, close-ups and positioning. His decisions must be the right ones as the programme is broadcast live, and any mistakes will appear on the television screens of millions of viewers.*

THE PRODUCTION ASSISTANT

The PA is really the director's assistant. PA's work very closely with the director both in the studio and on location. Before a programme even gets on air, the PA must do a lot of organizing and arranging — such as obtaining film and video tapes that need to be inserted into the programme and then timing all the 'inserts' to see how long they last. The PA also compiles all the information that appears in the credits at the beginning or end of the programme.

During both recorded and live shows, PA's sit in the gallery with a script and running order and count out loud how many minutes or seconds remain on each event. This is heard by everyone in the studio so that they know when an event is about to end and the next about to start. If something in the programme turns out to be shorter or longer than it was in rehearsals, the PA has to quickly recalculate timings during the show. This can be extremely hectic and the PA needs to be a calm person who doesn't panic under pressure.

THE VISION MIXER

The vision mixer physically presses the buttons that change the pictures we see on our television sets. In the gallery there are a number of monitors which show the pictures coming from all the studio cameras, material played back from video tape recording machines (VTR machines) and slides (stills). On instructions from the director, the vision mixer switches the picture we see at home from one camera to another, or to a slide or a recording. The vision mixer also creates any special effects such as fading (mixing) one picture into another, or making an actor appear to fly, even when he or she might be sitting in a studio.

THE MAKE-UP ARTIST

Everyone who appears on television needs to wear make-up. The lights in the studio are so bright that without make-up, people's skin looks too pale or too red.

It is the job of the make-up artist to make sure that the actors' or presenters' skin looks good on screen and that the make-up is applied evenly and subtly. Everyone's skin is different, so numerous techniques have to be used to make them look good.

The make-up artists' work is very varied. Sometimes they have to work with famous and well-known personalities, or make people up with weird colours and special effects for science-fiction programmes. Styles of make-up change as fashions evolve. Make-up artists need to know all about the history of make-up so that they can transform actors into people from any period in time.

Once they have applied make-up to all the performers, the make-up artists have to wait in the studio in case they are needed to 'touch up' — apply powder or rouge to performers who often sweat under the studio lights and whose skin becomes shiny.

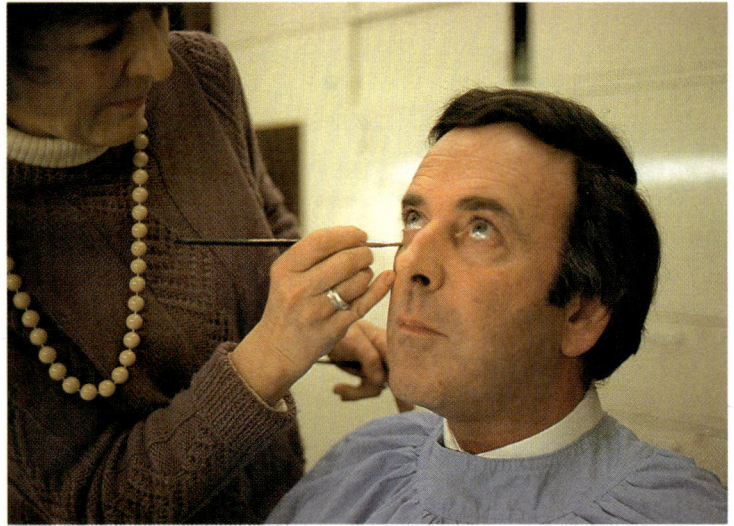

▲ A make-up artist adds the finishing touches to Terry Wogan's make-up before he appears on screen.

So you want to be a make-up artist?

● When watching television, look closely at the make-up that everyone is wearing. Try and imagine how the make-up artists achieve the different effects.

● Take part in school plays helping out with the make-up.

● Experiment on yourself and your friends.

● There are a number of courses available — mostly privately run.

▲ Actor Nedjet Salih plays café owner Ali Osman in Eastenders. Nedjet is being made up to look as if he has been in a fight for a scene in the series. The make-up artist is actually 'giving' him a black eye.

THE WARDROBE ASSISTANT

Every television programme needs someone to take care of all the wardrobe requirements. Costume and clothing varies from programme to programme. For example, a news reader traditionally wears smart, sensible clothes to reflect the serious nature of the subject, whereas, for a complicated period drama, the actors may need hundreds of elaborate costumes.

Wardrobe departments are kept very busy looking after all the programmes made by their company. As well as ordering clothes from specialist costume hirers, wardrobe assistants will make many of the clothes themselves. They also go shopping with actors and presenters to help them choose suitable clothes to wear on screen.

Wardrobe assistants have to check everything worn by performers before they go on screen. There are certain colours and designs that can cause problems. White clothes can actually 'flare' – they reflect the light and almost shine on camera. Certain checked patterns and closely-striped clothes 'strobe' on camera – the patterns move together causing a distracting colour sequence. Presenters who wear all black against a black back-drop, for example, will almost disappear and submerge with the background. Wardrobe assistants have to be constantly aware of what will look good and what will not.

They also have to possess a fairly detailed knowledge of the history of costumes and clothes.

▲ The unbelievably outrageous Dame Edna Everage, played by the Australian actor Barry Humphries, has an extensive array of wigs, costume jewellery and outfits. The wardrobe assistant who is responsible for selecting Dame Edna's wardrobe must have quite an original, and even bizarre, imagination.

THE SET DESIGNER

Every programme has a designer working on it who is responsible for all the scenery. On a small programme, such as a news programme, the scenery or 'set' may be quite straightforward, whereas on a drama or studio programme, the sets may be quite detailed.

Set designers have the daily challenge of trying to create, down to the most minute detail, sets from a particular period of history or that depict a particular scene. After making rough sketches of the set for the producer to approve, the designer then draws up a detailed plan which fits the shape and size of the studio. The designer then arranges for set builders, or carpenters, to actually build the sets. Sometimes sets are built in

▲ *Martin Horton is a set designer and set builder. Here, he is in his studio busily working out a set design for a forthcoming BBC series.*

the studio and then dismantled afterwards. More often, however, they are built so they can literally be wheeled in and out of the studio.

As television programmes become more advanced, so set design becomes more elaborate and adventurous. This gives set designers more artistic freedom, but, at the same time, requires them to devise more and more complicated sets. Some programmes actually alter their set design from week to week, which means that designers are continually having to work out variations to the sets.

This rough sketch is ▶ *of the Fowler family's living room in Eastenders.*
It was drawn in 1984 when the series was still at the planning stage. Do you think this initial sketch bears any resemblance to the room in the actual programme?

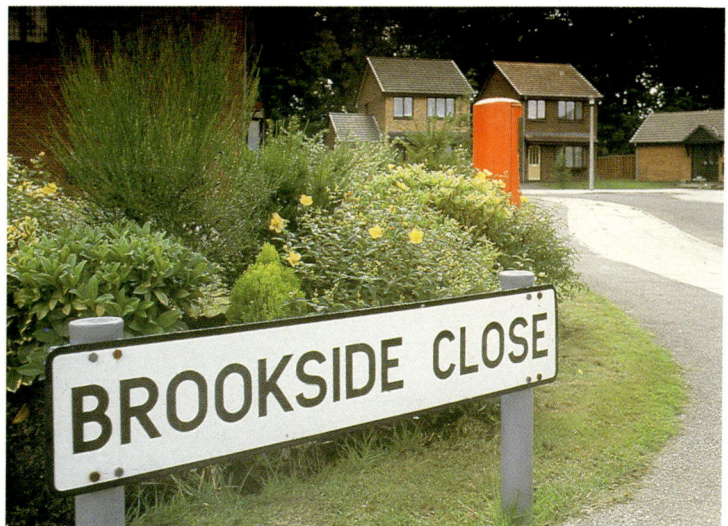

So you want to be a set designer?

● Watch television programmmes very carefully, paying close attention to the scenery and the amount of detail that has gone into it. For instance, in a sitcom (comedy set in a real-life situation) or soap opera, designers have to recreate a 'typical' scene with which the audience will be familiar. See if you can spot anything designers may have forgotten on particular programmes, or if you think something in the set looks out of place.

● Help out in school plays with props or set building.

● Polytechnics and colleges of higher or further education offer a variety of design-related courses. If you are interested, talk to your school careers officer.

▲ *A familiar scene — Brookside Close from the Channel 4 soap opera. The set — a cul-de-sac in Liverpool — looks totally realistic, but, although the houses are real, the insides are sets that are specially put together for the series. Some of the main rooms stay the same throughout, but others, such as the upstairs of the Corkhills' or Collins' houses become a lawyer's office or a doctor's surgery — whatever the particular scene demands.*

THE COMPUTER GRAPHICS DESIGNER

Television programmes have to continually change and evolve to keep pace with modern technology. One area of television that is having to change very rapidly is graphics.

Only a few years ago the graphic requirements of a programme would have been just a simple weather map drawn on card or paper. Today, however, the amount of artwork and graphic drawings needed on programmes has become extremely diverse and complicated. Most graphics seen on our televisions are created on computers. Computer graphics designers often study graphic design (design of books, magazines etc) and then go on to computer graphics.

There are two particular computers that are most commonly used: ASTON is used for the written words that appear on screen during a programme, called captions. When a caption moves across the screen it is called a crawling caption, and when it appears without moving it is called a static caption. PAINTBOX is the second computer graphics system. It is a very sophisticated system that allows the operator to create some stunning animated pictures. ITV's *The Chart Show* uses graphics instead of presenters. This lively music programme plays the latest pop records accompanied by videos. The sequences are linked by animated graphics and all the information about the artists or records is presented to the viewers in a series of captions. Computer graphics work very well for this particular type of programme – it can be very annoying if a presenter talks during your favourite record.

Computer graphics designers also create the title sequences that begin and end a programme. These vary enormously from programme to programme. Some have simple opening title sequences, whereas others use complicated computer-drawn animation. The designers also type the end credits into the ASTON computer system. The end credits are a list of names that shows who was involved in making the particular programme, including the actors, producers, directors, designers, camera crew and sound and lighting engineers. You can tell how difficult it has been to make a programme from the number of people who appear on the end credits.

So you want to be a computer graphics designer?

● You will need to be very talented at art and also be computer literate (able to understand and operate computers). Become involved in your school magazine — think of how the design could be improved.

● If you are very interested in art and creating images, then try to recreate those images on a computer screen. Certain computers can 'paint' pictures much more easily and quickly than can be done by hand on paper. Most schools and libraries have computers. There are also a wide number of courses available which will train you to use computers effectively. Private courses can be quite expensive, so try to get a computer teacher at school to teach you.

● Polytechnics and colleges of further and higher education offer art courses that involve graphic design and computer graphics design.

▲ *A computer graphics designer at work in front of her computer. Computer graphics design is a modern, fashionable art form.*

The logo from ITV's popular music programme The Chart Show. *The headphones and caption were designed and drawn on a computer.* ▼

CHAPTER THREE

IN THE STUDIO

Filming a scene from Eastenders, which is shot on location in Elstree, outside London. The large white screens on the left are used by the camera crew to help focus all the light on to the actual scene that is being filmed. They also help to distribute the light evenly.

THE CAMERA CREW

Most television camera crews work both in the studio and on location. Their work is very varied – for example, on a news programme or chat show, the studio cameras remain in the same position for the whole programme, whereas on a live music show, such as *Top of the Pops*, the camera crew have to move around quickly to get exciting pictures of the bands and the audience.

Camera crews who have to go on location can have very exciting jobs, especially if they are involved in a wildlife programme which means travelling to exotic places. Some camera crews have to travel to war zones to take 'on the spot' pictures of fighting — this can be dangerous and traumatic.

In the studio, the camera crew have to wear headsets through which they are given instructions by the director. The director tells them which angles to get and which positions to assume. During rehearsals the camera crew and the director try to work out details of positions and shots. They make notes on the camera script which is on a clipboard attached to the actual cameras. Coloured tape is stuck to the floor to mark out the particular positions the crew are meant to be in. The camera crew have to keep the picture in focus at all times, so that viewers do not get blurred images on their television sets. They also have to zoom in when instructed by the director to get close-up shots of the action.

The way in: Duncan Cross works as part of a camera crew for ITV. He says: *'It took me five years to get my job as part of a studio camera crew. I left school at eighteen and worked part-time in an office while going to college in the evening to study electronics. Three years later, I went on a special course in camera techniques. But, because it's the sort of job that lots of people want to do, I had to write lots of letters to television companies before I got the job. I also have a very keen interest in photography — that helps, too.'*

So you want to be part of a camera crew?

- GCSE maths and physics would be more than helpful to have. They would show you are technically minded — television cameras are very complicated pieces of equipment.
- Develop an interest in photography so you know what sort of picture will look interesting and also about the lighting needed to take particular pictures.

Filming a rugby league game. The camera person shelters under a cover so as to be able to concentrate solely on the action, and not have outside distractions interfering with the line of vision. ▼

▲ A rehearsal for the Central Television quiz show The Price is Right. *The lights on the ceiling can be moved up and down depending on how much light is needed. They are positioned so that different parts of the studio can receive different amounts of light.*

THE LIGHTING ENGINEER

If you have ever taken a photograph in a dark room without a flash, you will no doubt know that the outcome will be a dark picture with virtually no details. The same is true in television, where cameras often require more light than usual.

A lighting engineer's job is very complex. Apart from ensuring that there is always adequate light for the particular production, he or she must actually position the lights so that there are no shadows, particularly from cameras, floor managers, sound booms, staff and pieces of equipment. Lighting engineers must move and position the bright studio lamps and fix each one to an electrical hoist. This means that each lamp can be lowered to the studio floor at the touch of a button and adjusted as required. Lighting can create different moods and effects, for example, if a scene in a play is set at night-time it must be dark. However, if it were truly dark the viewer would not be able to see anything at all. In this case the lighting engineer might use a lot of blue light with a single lamp to create moonlight.

During a programme, the lighting engineer sits in the lighting gallery, from where all the studio lamps and their brightness can be adjusted by remote control.

26

THE SOUND ENGINEER

The sound that comes from our television sets is just as important as the visual images. There is not much point in watching someone speak if we cannot hear what they are saying. It is the job of the sound engineers to make sure that what we hear is always of good quality and not muffled or distorted.

The mood of any programme can be changed by adding music and sound effects. For example, adding the sound of a harp playing could make a scene appear magical or dream-like, whereas playing a fast disco record can make a programme appear to be slick and fast-moving. Of course, if these sounds were as loud as the actors' or presenters' voices we might not be able to hear what they were saying. It is the responsibility of the sound engineer at the control desk to make sure the mix of sounds is correct. It is the sound department's responsibility to carefully position microphones in the studio.

A sound engineer at work mixing in the sounds for the BBC I weekly sports programme Grandstand. The engineer has a list of instructions which tell him at which points in the programme he must mix in music and any other sounds that are required. ▼

THE STAGE MANAGER

On any television programme there are always a number of props that have to be ordered, arranged and put in position in the studio.

Depending on the type of production the stage manager is working on, he or she can have either very few or literally hundreds of props to co-ordinate. On a programme such as *The Wogan Show*, there are few props — only a vase of flowers and perhaps a couple of ornaments. However, the stage manager must choose the ornaments carefully. The viewer must always concentrate on the guest and presenter of a news or chat show programme, the props must never distract attention. For other programmes, where the props and scenery are an integral part of the action, they must look completely in place and realistic. A programme like *Neighbours* needs lots of props to recreate the insides of typical Australian houses.

The researcher or the producer will give the stage manager a list of the props that are needed for the programme about one week in advance. For a modern soap opera or sitcom, this usually does not create many problems, although it can be difficult to get the exact props to suit what the director has in mind. A production such as a period drama can prove a nightmare for stage managers, who might have to come up with pieces of antique furniture. Sometimes specialist props can be hired from prop companies but, more often than not, stage managers have to spend a lot of their time researching where and how particular items can be found.

Stage managers have a number of stage hands to help them position the props and move them about, if necessary.

Behind the scenes of Grandstand. Television has become such a fast-moving and professional business that programme-making looks extremely easy. Viewers often do not appreciate the panic and mayhem that is going on off-screen, especially on live programmes, when if something goes wrong it cannot be cut or reshot. People who choose a career in the television industry opt for jobs that are varied, interesting and extremely pressurized. ▼

THE FLOOR MANAGER

The floor manager, as the name suggests, is in charge of the studio floor and everything that goes on there, especially during a broadcast. He or she communicates with the gallery through a headset.

It is the floor manager's responsibility to pass information from the production assistant, the director and the producer to people on the studio floor. This information might involve cues for actors or presenters – letting them know who is on next. The floor manager also has to give a number of hand signals which let the people on camera know how much time they have left, how long there is before a commercial, whether to cut an item short or make it stretch out for a bit longer. He or she is also responsible for giving similar instructions to other studio staff – the stage manager, stage hands and the camera crew, for example.

The floor manager has to go through floor plans and scripts with the director before going on air. Together they work out all the studio manoeuvres. Floor managers are also responsible for safety; they must ensure that all fire regulations are enforced.

▲ *The floor manager (on the right) is instructing the camera crew about which shots to take. The floor manager has to be on hand at all times to let presenters and actors know how much time is left, and also to pass on information from the director and producer to people on the studio floor.*

29

G L O S S A R Y

Ad lib   Having to carry on talking or talk spontaneously when you have already said everything that had been rehearsed.

Audition   A test at which performers are asked to demonstrate their ability to sing, dance, act or present etc, to judge whether or not they are suitable for a particular role.

Commission   Officially asking someone to do something. In television, people are commissioned to devise or produce a programme.

Cue   A sign, often verbal, that it is someone's turn to do or say something.

Monitors   A number of screens in a television studio which show all the programmes on each different channel and the film being shot by each studio camera.

Period drama   A programme set during a particular time in history.

Programme format   The basic outline of a television programme which shows who the different characters are and what they are like. It also outlines how the programme will be structured.

Running order   An outline of the timing and sequence of events of any television programme.

Science fiction   Stories concerning space and the future.

Soap opera   A long-running series, such as *Coronation Street, Brookside, Eastenders* or *Neighbours,* which focuses on the day-to-day lives of ordinary people.

Technology   Advanced scientific methods.

F U R T H E R   R E A D I N G

BBC Annual Report and Handbook (BBC, annual).
Learning the Media by Manuel Alvarado, Robin Gutch and Tana Wollen (Macmillan, 1987).
Television and Radio (IBA, annual).
Television and Video by Manuel Alvarado (Wayland, 1987).
The Guinness Book of Superlatives by Kenneth Parringham (Guinness Superlatives, 1984).

PICTURE ACKNOWLEDGEMENTS

The Publisher would like to thank the following for providing the pictures used in this book: BBC/BBC Enterprises 9, 11, 12, 13, 18 (bottom), 19, 21 (top), 24; Channel 4 TV 5, 10 (bottom), 15, 21 (bottom), 23 (bottom); London Features International COVER, 6, 10 (top), 14 (both); Paul Seheult 7, 20, 23 (top); Topham Picture Library 8, 17, 18 (bottom), 25, 26, 27, 28, 29.

I N D E X

The numbers in **bold** refer to captions